Traditional British Cooking
with Coloured Images for every Recipe.
Enjoy Delicious and Easy Meals

WILLOW MORRIS

Copyright 2022 by Willow Morris - All rights reserved.
The following Book is reproduced below with the goal of providing information that is as accurate and reliable as possible. Regardless, purchasing this Book can be seen as consent to the fact that both the publisher and the author of this book are in no way experts on the topics discussed within and that any recommendations or suggestions that are made herein are for entertainment purposes only. Professionals should be consulted as needed prior to undertaking any of the action endorsed herein.

This declaration is deemed fair and valid by both the American Bar Association and the Committee of Publishers Association and is legally binding throughout the United States.

Furthermore, the transmission, duplication, or reproduction of any of the following work including specific information will be considered an illegal act irrespective of if it is done electronically or in print. This extends to creating a secondary or tertiary copy of the work or a recorded copy and is only allowed with the express written consent from the Publisher. All additional right reserved.

The information in the following pages is broadly considered a truthful and accurate account of facts and as such, any inattention, use, or misuse of the information in question by the reader will render any resulting actions solely under their purview. There are no scenarios in which the publisher or the original author of this work can be in any fashion deemed liable for any hardship or damages that may befall them after undertaking information described herein.

Additionally, the information in the following pages is intended only for informational purposes and should thus be thought of as universal. As befitting its nature, it is presented without assurance regarding its prolonged validity or interim quality. Trademarks that are mentioned are done without written consent and can in no way be considered an endorsement from the trademark holder.

TABLE OF CONTENTS

INTRODUCTION 5

    Advantages to Using an Air Fryer 5

    Various Types of Air Fryers and How to Choose the One for You 9

    Two Common Differences 9

    Accessory Tools for Air Fryer Cooking 11

    How To Clean An Air Fryer 13

Chapter 1: BREAKFAST RECIPES 14

Chapter 2: MAIN DISH RECIPES 25

Chapter 3: SIDE DISH RECIPES 59

Chapter 4: DESSERTS 75

RECIPES INDEX 87

INTRODUCTION

Air Fryers have started to become popular, due to the fact that you can avoid many of the unhealthy aspects of modern cooking. But what is an Air Fryer exactly, and how on earth does it work?

Air Fryers are basically an upgraded, enhanced countertop oven, but they became popular for one particular reason. In fact, many of the manufacturers, such as Philips, market this machine solely based on the claim that the Air Fryers accurately mimic deep-frying, which, although extremely unhealthy, is still very popular in this day and age (as it is, in my opinion, one of the most delicious ways to eat food).

Air Fryers work with the use of a fan and a heating mechanism. You place the food you want cooked in a basket or on the rack, turn on the machine, and the Air Fryer distributes oven-temperature hot air around your food. It provides consistent, pervasive heat evenly to all the food within.

This heat circulation achieves the crispy taste and texture that is so tantalizing in deep fried foods, but without the unhealthy and dangerous oil! Both have been replaced by this miracle machine with hot air and a fan.

Advantages to Using an Air Fryer

I may have already slipped in a few of the advantages to using an Air Fryer, but now let's expand a little more on everything an Air Fryer can do for you. After all, no investment should be made unless it's absolutely worthwhile.

And in truth, the Air Fryer is very worthwhile. I cannot begin to tell you how the advantages start piling up; this is not just another average appliance that everyone is getting because of a simple trend. People are getting Air Fryers because of their incredible, numerous, multifaceted benefits. There are, however, a few notable advantages of using an Air Fryer, which I'll list below. If you don't know anything else about Air Fryers, I hope that these will convince you of their worth.

Healthier Cooking

This is perhaps the top benefit that comes with air frying. In a society that really struggles with healthy cooking, we can use all the help we can get. Luckily, Air Fryers make it easy, all while maintaining many of the factors that make unhealthy food delicious!

Air Fryers use very little oil, which is one of the best ways to replace those unhealthy fried foods, like fried chicken, potatoes, and so many others. If you are like me (a lover of deep fried foods) then this is the answer to your dilemma of healthy eating while still enjoying the crispy taste of food!

Do keep in mind that you still need to spray fried foods, such as fish, with a touch of oil to make sure it does get evenly crispy. All in all, however, there is no denying the amount of oils is a whole lot less.

This singular change makes all the difference in the world. Healthy eating has never been easier, as you'll get the same crispy and flavoursome results, with minimal amounts of added oils. You'll even be able to "fry" foods you never were able to before—the possibilities are endless!

Safer and Easier

Nothing scares me more than a hot pot of oil. It is an accident waiting to happen, and getting struck with burning oil splatters is no joke! But this, and its corresponding injuries, is often the price to pay for deep fried foods.

Air Fryers are also user-friendly, and this makes a huge difference. You don't have to feel like you are studying for a degree when working with an Air Fryer. Making dinner is far less complicated in an Air Fryer than many of the traditional methods of cooking. For some meals—unless you choose one of the more complex recipes I'll share later—you can even revert to placing a small piece of meat (even if it happens to be frozen!) into the basket and select the cooking settings.

The simplicity of the Air Fryer is its beauty. You will save countless time and unnecessary frustrations, and still make delicious food!

Faster Than Cooking in the Oven

Once you buy an Air Fryer and set it to heat for the first time, you won't know what hit you! The average normal oven needs about 10 minutes to preheat. Due to the Air Fryer's smaller size and innovative design, it will be ready to go in no time!

It's even faster during the actual cooking. With the circulation that allows your food to be cooked crisp and even, it cuts a whole lot of Cooking out of the equation. This is amazing, especially in this day and age where technology, work, friends, family, and even pets are constantly demanding our attention.

Just imagine! You could set your food in the Air Fryer, and (with some recipes) it will be ready to eat in less than 20 minutes!

Saves Space

If you are someone living in a small apartment, or a student accommodation, then an Air Fryer is perfect for you. Air Fryers are much smaller in comparison to a conventional oven and you can easily make use of this Air Fryer in 1 cubic foot of your kitchen.

You can even pack your Air Fryer away after use if need be, but the majority of people choose to keep it out on the counter. But it's nice to have the option to move your Air Fryer around if space becomes an issue.

Low Operating Costs

Considering how much cooking oil costs these days and the amount you need to use, you will soon be cutting costs in making deep fried foods. All an Air Fryer uses is a small amount of oil and some of the electricity to power up the Air Fryer, about the same amount that a countertop oven would.

Not only will you be cutting out the massive oil costs, which will save money, you will likely also save money by ordering out less, as you'll be able to replicate your favourite foods quickly and easily at home!

No Oil Smell

In reality, smelling like the food you just ate is not impressive, regardless of how delicious the food may be. This is what often happens, however, when people enjoy deep fried foods.

When deep frying foods, it also causes the whole house to smell, and as the oil splatters around, it can leave a massive mess. The oil can even harden on the walls, causing grime to build up into a nasty concentration of dirt and grease.

With less cooking oil, Air Fryers don't have any of those oil smells and keeps the space cleaner around you, as all the oils, smells, and actual cooking are contained within the machine.

Preserves Nutrients

When you are cooking your food in an Air Fryer, it actually protects a lot of the food from losing all its moisture. This means that with the use of a little oil, as well as circulation with hot air, it can allow your food to keep most of its nutrients which is excellent for you! If you want to cook healthy foods with the purpose of maintaining as many nutrients as possible, then an Air Fryer is perfect for you!

Easier to Clean

Cleaning is perhaps the bane of my existence, especially after cooking and having a long day. This can really take away a lot of the pleasure of making yourself a great meal. But an Air Fryer lightens the burden by being easy to clean!

Consistent cleaning after using it (much like any pot or pan) can allow for easier and simpler living. You just need some soapy water and a non-scratch sponge to clean both the exterior and the interior of your Air Fryer. Some Air Fryers are even dishwasher-safe!

Great Flavour

The flavour of Air Fryer "fried" foods is nearly identical to traditional frying, and the texture is exact. You can cook a lot of those great frozen foods, such as onion rings or french fries, and still achieve that crunchy effect. This certainly can help you turn to healthier foods, especially if your goal is for healthy but quality meals.

The Air Fryer helps to cook your food to perfect crispness, instead of the soggy mess that happens when you try alternative methods of cooking foods that are meant to be deep fried (like chicken tenders). No one really enjoys mushy food. The Air Fryer keeps that desired element while remaining healthy.

All you will really need is just some cooking oil sprayed outside of your food to end up with a cooked interior and a crunchy exterior. So no worries! You still can eat your foods with a crunch and a healthier result!

Versatile

Unlike rice cookers meant just for rice, or bread makers meant just for bread, you will find that an Air Fryer leaves a lot of room to be both versatile and healthier. You can cook almost anything you would like in the Air Fryer (as long as it fits). From spaghetti squash, to desserts, even to fried chicken! You will probably never run out of air frying options!

Various Types of Air Fryers and How to Choose the One for You

There isn't one standardized choice of Air Fryers, which means you are far more likely to find an Air Fryer that really suits your particular needs. Whether it be size or price, you have a wider variety of choices than what normally comes with conventional ovens.

So what are the key aspects that you need to take into consideration when getting yourself a nice Air Fryer? Let's begin:

Dimensions: Obviously they come in different sizes, and despite saving space, some can still be bulky. When thinking about your countertop, you do want to consider its size and dimensions. You don't want to play a game of tilt with your Air Fryer, nor have it taken up all the extra space you have!

Safety Features: You may want to check that it has an auto shutoff, as it is certainly a desirable feature. Air Fryers can get very hot during use, and an auto-shutoff can save you a lot of stress and fire emergencies. Furthermore, having a cool exterior can prevent potential red and burnt hands. So do yourself a favor and make sure they have all these elements at hand.

Reviews: Naturally, this is the best thing to check out. Considering that the businesses rarely give out all the information, you will certainly find it out when people leave reviews. The customer hides nothing, and if they are unhappy, they make sure everyone else knows about it.

However, if people are very happy, many of them will also note it in the reviews, and it is best to target the Air Fryers that tend to have the high reviews.

Two Common Differences

Beyond those functional differences, there are two mainstream designs of Air Fryers: basket Air Fryers and oven Air Fryers. Each has very unique and distinguished features in which to enjoy. Let us take a look at the differences between the two:

Basket Air Fryers

Basket fryers are known to need less space than oven Air Fryers, which is very practical if you have limited space. Not only does it save space, but it also saves time, as the food is quickly heated up (without unnecessarily heating up the kitchen). Unlike an oven Air Fryer, and the larger traditional oven, it only takes about 1-2 minutes for the basket Air Fryer to heat up, and it is quite easy to place the foods inside of the basket.

The cons are, for one, that it does make a lot more noise than the oven Air Fryer. You also will not be able to watch the food as it cooks, which can increase the chances of burnt food if you are not careful. Also, a basket Air Fryer may not be the best if you need to cook a lot of food, as it is limited in capacity. This means that batch cooking may be required if you need a large amount of food.

This makes a basket Air Fryer ideal if you have a limited budget, don't need to cook a huge amount of food, and have limited free time. They are quick, small, and convenient, especially perfect for people who are students or single working professionals, and maybe even you!

Oven Air Fryers

Oven Air Fryers, in contrast, have a larger capacity, which means you can cook a lot more food at the same time. They also have multiple functions for cooking and cut down on the noise than the basket Air Fryer. You will also be able to move the food closer or even further away from the heating element. There is a lot more flexibility involved in the use of an oven Air Fryer. Best of all, you can place parts of the oven Air Fryer into the dishwasher to be washed (thus cutting down the cleaning process, if you happen to have a dishwasher).

But, do be aware that it takes up more counter space, and takes a larger initial bite out of your wallet. It may also heat up the kitchen more, and if you are in fashion and aesthetic design, it might be disappointing to find out the colors and themes are more limited than basket Air Fryers.

These are the two main common types of Air Fryers; however, there are new types of Air Fryers that are coming to light for you to use and enjoy, most notably, the paddle-type Air Fryer. This version has a paddle that moves through the basket of your Air Fryer in order to help circulate hot air in between each piece of food. This saves you the effort of pulling your food out at a specific time and shaking or stirring it. These can also be noisy, and heat up the space, and are not small and convenient; however, if you are someone looking for convenience, then this is the Air Fryer to go for.

Accessory Tools for Air Fryer Cooking

I love how Air Fryers save time, so I've compiled a list of my favourite time-saving tools that I often use when meal prepping with my Air Fryer. Anything to help make your life easier and healthier should certainly be considered, and what better way to help than by adding some accessories to your Air Fryer inventory?

Mandoline

Preparation is always needed before jumping into air frying, and getting yourself the mandoline slicer is the perfect tool to slice online rings, pickles, or even the best and crunchiest chips. You can select the thickness or thinness, depending on what the recipe needs and says, so you will always be able to get the perfect crispness.

Grill Pan

This is simply a pan created with a perforated surface. With this tool, you can both grill and sear foods like fish or even vegetables inside your Air Fryer. They are also commonly non-stick, which really helps your overall cleanup.

However, before you purchase a grill pan, make sure the Air Fryer model you have does support the grill pan. The last thing you want is to find that your grill pan just does not fit inside your Air Fryer.

Heat Resistant Tongs

There is no denying how hot an Air Fryer can get inside, and unless you are a superhero, you will need some help maneuvering in foods in and outside of the basket if need be.

Using heat-resistant tongs can really make your life infinitely easier by keeping your foods, and your hands, safe. They are affordable, and really useful to allow for an even cooking process.

Air Fryer Liners

If you'd like to further decrease your clean-up time, then this is for you! These liners are both non-stick and non-toxic, making this a classic little investment for you to consider. They prevent the food from sticking to your Air Fryer and help in the process of keeping your little machine clean. You will not have to worry about burnt foods inside your fryer again!

Air Fryer Rack
This adds a little bit more versatility as you can really take advantage of the surface cooking. With a rack, you ensure that heat is evenly distributed to all 360 degrees of your food. They are very safe and easy to use, and they increase the number of dishes you can cook at the same time

Baking Pans
With an Air Fryer, you can even bake! You just need the right equipment, such as a barrel or round pan. With this you can even bake pizza, bread, muffins, and more. Imagine telling people you baked your own cake with an Air Fryer!

Silicone Baking Cups
From egg bites to muffins, these are individual cups you can use in order to help compensate for the smaller space within an Air Fryer.

The silicone material is heat-resistant, and allows for easier release of the contents, which spares you a lot of time cleaning. If you are a fan of baking, then this is a must have.

Oil Sprayer
Naturally, one of the top benefits is needing much less oil when cooking with an Air Fryer, but it does not necessarily mean that you can cook with no oil at all.

An oil sprayer is the key to getting the food you want to that nice golden-brown. You can use any oil that you like to use when cooking; all you need is a little spritz before you close the machine, and you are set!

Thermapen
Having the right Cooking is very important, but temperature also counts for a lot, and this is a nice little accessory to add to your collection. Having an instant-read thermometer can ensure all the food you have is cooked (and evenly so).

If you are not completely certain at what temperatures food should be, you can always check out the various different guides.

How To Clean An Air Fryer

As mentioned before, an Air Fryer is really easy to clean, but that doesn't mean you'll never need to clean it! Also, please remember that the cleanliness of your machine depends on how often you use it, and what you use it for.

It is recommended that you clean your Air Fryer after every use. As tempting as it may be to skip a day, it really is not worth it over the long run.

And that is the first step that comes with cleaning an Air Fryer:

Do not delay the cleaning. Simply don't. Allowing crumbs or random bits of food to harden overnight can turn an easy task into a nightmare of a chore. If you do happen to air-fry foods that come with a form of sticky sauce, then the warmer they are, the easier again they will be to clean and remove.

Unplug the machine, and use warm and soapy water to properly remove the dirt and components. You do not want anything abrasive in there. If there is food that gets stuck, try soaking it until it is soft enough to remove. If there is any food that happens to be stuck on the grate or in the basket, then you should consider gently using a toothpick or even a wooden skewer to scrape it off, in order to be thorough with your cleaning process.

Remember to wipe the inside with a damp, soapy cloth, and remember to remove both the drawer and the basket.

Finally, wipe the outside of your Air Fryer with a damp cloth or a sponge.

If there are any odors that seem to be stuck to your Air Fryer after cooking a strong food, even after you have cleaned it, then you can consider using a product called NewAir.

Just soak it in with water for about 30 minutes to an hour before you clean it. If the smell remains, then rub one lemon half over the drawer and the basket. Allow it to soak for another 30 minutes before washing it again.

Please do be careful with any non-stick appliances. They are a wonder for cleaning, but they can flake or come off over time. Be gentle, as you do not want anything to scratch or to even chip the coating. Not only does it ruin a little bit of the aesthetic look, a small part of your Air Fryer will constantly be struggling with sticky food.

There you have it! The first stepping stones and foundational knowledge of an Air Fryer. The device you will choose, and how you will use it is up to you, but there are still so many exciting varieties, choices, and options to come!

Chapter 1

BREAKFAST RECIPES

Fried Bacon

Prep Time: 2 mins
Cooking Time: 8 mins
Servings: 3

Directions
1. Place the bacon slices in a single layer of the air fryer tray or in the basket.
2. Cook for 8 - 10 minutes at 200°C. There is no need to preheat
3. Depending on the thickness of the bacon the cooking time may vary, so check as you go along whether it is cooked to the point you want

Nutrition: Calories: 118kcal; Protein: 21g; Fat: 4g

Ingredients
> 1 pack Back Bacon

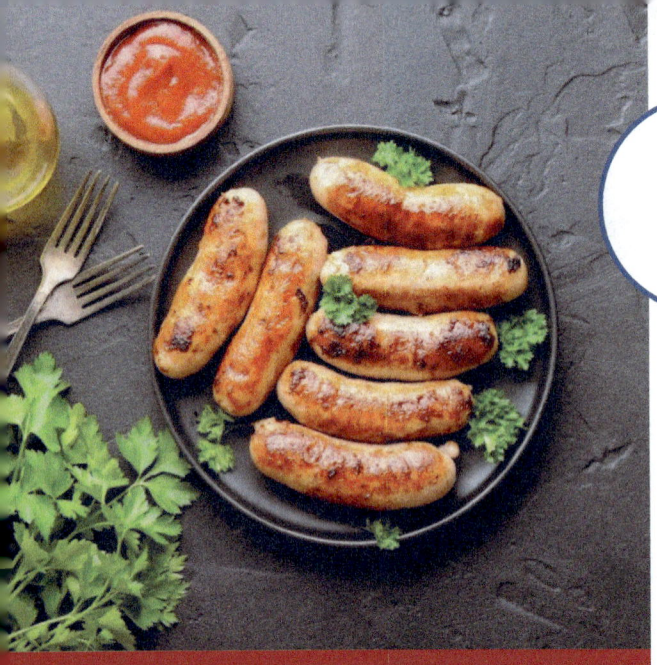

Sausages in Air Fryer

Prep Time: 5 mins
Cooking Time: 12 mins
Servings: 6

Ingredients
- 6 Sausages
- 3 squirts Spray Oil

Directions
1. Preheat your air fryer to 180°C for 5 minutes
2. Prick each sausage a couple of times (you can use a knife or fork).
3. Spray the bottom of the air fryer with a few splashes of oil to prevent the sausages from sticking.
4. Use the tongs to gently insert the sausages (do not let them touch so that they cook evenly).
5. Set timer to 12 minutes (adjust the time for small, large or frozen sausages).
6. Halfway through cooking, turn with tongs.
7. Check after 12 minutes and reheat if necessary.Serve with your chosen meal

Nutrition: Calories: 209kcal; Carbohydrates: 2g; Protein: 11g; Fat: 17g

Air Fryer Boiled Eggs

Prep Time: 1 Minute
Cooking Time: 10 Minutes
Servings: 4

Directions
1. Place room temperature eggs in the basket of the air fryer, leaving space between the eggs to allow the hot air to circulate. Use a metal rack to fit more, if necessary.
2. Set the air fryer to 150°C. Cook according your preferences (from 8 minutes for soft-boiled eggs to 12 minutes for hard-boiled eggs).
3. Once cooked, remove from the airfryer basket and place in an ice bath or bowl of cold water. This will prevent the eggs from continuing to cook. When it's cool and safe to touch, remove the skin.

Nutrition: Calories: 72; Fat: 5g; Carbohydrates: 0g; Fibre: 0g; Sugar: 0g; Protein: 6g

Ingredients
- 4 eggs (use as many as you want)

Scotch Eggs

Prep Time: 15 minutes
Cooking Time: 12 minutes
Servings: 6

Ingredients
- 6 boiled eggs peeled
- 1 packet 400g Powters Sausagemeat
- 30 g Flour
- ½ teaspoon garlic powder
- 1 large egg beaten
- 120 g Breadcrumbs
- 1 tablespoon brown sugar
- ½ smoked paprika

Directions
1. Divide the sausage into 6 equal portions and roll them into a balls
2. Place a sausage ball on your counter or parchment paper if you don't want to clean up later.
3. Pat the sausage balls until they reach the form of an oval big enough to hold an egg.
4. Place the peeled, boiled eggs in the center of the sausages patties and wrap the sausages around the eggs, applying pressure with your hands.
5. Now take 3 bowls and put, in order: flour and garlic powder combined, beaten egg, panko or breadcrumbs with brown sugar and smoked paprika.
6. Roll each sausage-covered egg in bowl 1, then dip in bowl 2 and coat in the breadcrumbs bowl.
7. Preheat your air fryer to 190°C for 10 min.
8. Place Scotch eggs in the air fryer basket, ensuring enough space between each other to let the air circulate.
9. Air fry the eggs for 12 minutes, evenly turning halfway through to brown.

Nutrition: Calories 396; Fat 27 g; Protein 29 g; Carbs 16 g; Fiber 1 g; Sugar 1 g;

Bacon Muffins

Prep Time: 7 minutes
Cooking Time: 6 minutes
Servings: 1

Directions
1. Crack the large egg into either a ramekin or oven proof dish
2. Slice the muffin in half
3. Layer 1 slice of burger cheese on 1 half
4. Place now the muffin and bacon in the Air Fryer drawer, place the ovenproof dish or ramekin in the drawer too.
5. Heat up the Air Fryer to 200°C for 6 minutes
6. Once is done, assemble the breakfast muffin and add the extra slice of cheese on top.

Nutrition: Calories: 291; Fat: 12 g; Protein: 15 g; Carbs: 25 g; Fibre: 2 g; Sugar: 0 g

Ingredients
- 1 Large Egg
- 1 Slice of Unsmoked Bacon
- 1 English All Butter Muffin
- 2 Slices of Burger Cheese
- 1 Pinch of Salt and Pepper

Sausage Sandwiches

Prep Time: 11 minutes
Cooking Time: 15 minutes
Servings: 4

Ingredients
- 4 breakfast sausage patties
- 4 eggs
- kosher salt, pepper
- 1 tbsp. butter
- 4 bagel thins or english muffins
- 4 slices cheese of choice

Directions
1. Lay the breakfast sausage patties in your Air Fryer basket. Set the Air Fryer to 200°C, 15 minutes.
2. Remove the sausage and lay on some paper towels to drain the excess fat.
3. Take a bowl and beat the eggs inside, add kosher salt and pepper. In a medium size skillet, medium low heat, add butter, once it's melted add beaten eggs in a single layer.
4. Cook 2-3 minutes and flip, cook one or two more minutes. Remove the eggs from the pan, cut into 4 equal pieces.
5. Lay the bottom part of the English muffin or the bagel in the Air Fryer basket. Add a sausage patty to each, top with the cooked egg and a slice of cheese.
6. Put the top of the english muffin or the bagel on each sandwich.
7. Set the Air Fryer to 200°C, 4 to 5 minutes.
8. Serve.

Nutrition: Calories: 323; Fat: 13 g; Protein: 22 g; Carbs: 29 g; Fibre: 4 g; Sugar: 1 g

Black Pudding (Packed)

Prep Time: 0 minutes
Cooking Time: 9 minutes
Servings: 2

Directions
1. If your black pudding is still frozen, air fry it in the air fryer for 6 minutes at 80°C, then it will be soft enough to cut.
2. Remove from the air fryer. Cut into slices, removing the wrapper.
3. Place the slices in the frying basket and cook at 180°C for 9 minutes.
4. Serve.

Nutrition: Calories: 297kcal; Fat: 22 g

Ingredients
- Black Pudding Slices

Vegetables Breakfast Frittata

Prep Time: 5 Minutes
Cooking Time: 10 Minutes
Servings: 2

Ingredients
- Oil or butter to grease the pan
- 3 eggs
- 1/4 red pepper, diced
- 1/4 green pepper, diced
- 10 baby spinach leaves, chopped
- Handful of cheddar cheese, grated
- Salt and pepper to season, optional

Directions
1. In a bowl, beat the eggs. Season with salt and pepper as needed. Grease a skillet with oil or butter and place it in the air fryer.
2. Switch to 180°C and heat for 1 minute. Add peppers and air fry for 3 minutes. Pour in the spinach and egg mixture. Sprinkle melted cheese on top.
3. Cook for another 6 minutes, making sure not to overcook halfway through.

Nutrition: Calories: 254; Fat: 15.5 g; Protein: 19 g; Carbs: 8.5 g; Fibre: 3.5 g; Sugar: 0.5 g

Cheese Omelette

Prep Time: 10 minutes
Cooking Time: 10 minutes
Servings: 1

Directions
1. In a medium mixing jug, combine the eggs and milk
2. Add the salt and garnishes and combine well
3. Take a 15x8 cm pan and grease well, before pouring the mixture inside
4. Arrange the pan inside the Air Fryer basket
5. Cook at 170ºC for 10 minutes
6. At the halfway point, sprinkle the cheese on top and loosen the edges with a spatula
7. Remove and enjoy!

Nutrition: Calories: 395; Fat: 27 g; Protein: 25 g; Carbs: 7 g; Fibre: 0 g; Sugar: 6 g

Ingredients
- 2 eggs
- 150 ml milk
- Pinch of salt
- 40g shredded cheese
- Any toppings you like, such as mushrooms, peppers, onions, etc

French Toast Sticks

Prep Time: 5 minutes
Cooking Time: 10 minutes
Servings: 6

Ingredients
- 3 tbsp. of caster sugar
- Salt
- 80 ml of double cream
- 1/4 tsp. of ground cinnamon
- 1/2 tsp. of vanilla extract
- 6 thick slices white loaf or brioche, each slice cut into thirds
- Maple syrup, for serving
- 2 large eggs
- 80 ml of whole milk

Directions
1. Take a large shallow baking dish and beat sugar, cream, eggs, cinnamon, vanilla, milk, and a pinch of salt.
2. Add bread, turn to coat for few times.
3. Arrange the french toast into the Air Fryer basket, working in batches to not overcrowd the basket. Set Air Fryer to 190°C, cook until golden, about 8 minutes, tossing halfway through.
4. Serve warm, drizzled with maple syrup.

Nutrition: Calories: 166; Fat: 7 g; Protein: 6 g; Carbs: 18 g; Fibre: 2.5 g; Sugar: 7 g

Chapter 2
MAIN DISH RECIPES

Tandoori Chicken Tikka Kebab

Prep Time: 10 mins
Cooking Time: 15 mins
Servings: 6

Equipment
› Wooden Kebab Sticks
›

Ingredients
› 2-3 Large Chicken Breast Cubed
› 4 tbsp Fat Free Yoghurt (or full fat)
› 2 tbsp Tandoori Masala Spice Blend Powder (or Garam Masala)
› 2 cloves Garlic Crushed
› 1 Lemon ½ for the juice, ½ sliced into wedges to serve
› Spray oil

Directions
1. When preparing chicken, it is best to soak the bamboo skewers in water. Cut them according to the size of the pan or tray you will be cooking with.
2. In a bowl or food bag, put the yoghurt, tandoori masala, garlic and the juice of half a lemon. Add the diced chicken breast and mix. For best results, let it marinate for two hours in the refrigerator. Thread the chicken onto kebab sticks. 4-6 chicken sticks are needed.
3. Preheat to 180°C for 5 minutes, add oil and fry for about 15 minutes. It is not necessary to flip halfway through cooking.

Optional: Sprinkle finely chopped coriander on top when serving.

Nutrition: Calories: 107kcal; Carbohydrates: 4g; Protein: 17g; Fat: 2g Fibre: 1g; Sugar: 1g

Chicken Drumsticks Italian Style

Prep Time: 10 mins
Cooking Time: 30 mins
Servings: 3

Directions

1. Place all the marinade ingredients in a ziplock bag or sandwich bag, seal and mix the ingredients with your fingers.
2. Bag the chicken thighs, mix with the marinade and cook immediately or marinate in the fridge for up to 2 hours.
3. Preheat the air fryer to 200°C. Place chicken drumstick in a single layer inside the Air fryer for 25 minutes (turning halfway)

Nutrition: Calories: 502kcal; Carbohydrates: 3 g; Protein: 27 g; Fat: 42 g; Fibre: 1 g; Sugar: 1 g

Equipment
› Zip bags

Ingredients
› 6 Chicken Drumsticks
› 6 tbsp Olive Oil
› 1 tbsp White Wine Vinegar
› 2 tsp Gia Garlic Puree
› 2 tsp Italian Seasonig
› 1 tsp Dark Brown Sugar
› 1/2 Lemon Juice
› 1 Lemon zest
› small handful Fresh Basil chopped

Chicken Wings in Air Fryer

Prep Time: 5 Minutes
Cooking Time: 25 Minutes
Servings: 4

Ingredients
- 1 kg chicken wings
- 1 tbsp olive oil
- ½ tsp garlic powder
- ½ tsp onion powder
- ½ tsp paprika
- ½ tsp salt
- ½ tsp black pepper

Directions
1. Preheat the air fryer to 180°C. First, dry the chicken wings with a paper towel.
2. Place the chicken wings in a large bowl, cover with olive oil and toss the wings to coat as much as possible. Add all the spices and coat all the wings.
3. Place the chicken wings in the air fryer. Depending on the number of wings to be cooked and the size of the air fryer, it may be necessary to do this in batches. You can also use the air fryer's rack to hold more, but above all make sure that the wings do not touch each other and that they have room to crisp up.
4. Cook for about 20 minutes, turning 2-3 times to ensure even cooking. Increase the temperature to 200°C and bake for a further 5 minutes or until the skin is crispy.
5. Serve with BBQ sauce, chilli sauce or Buffalo sauce.

Nutrition: Calories: 853; Fat: 64 g; Carbohydrates: 25 g; Fibre: 1 g; Sugar: 1 g; Protein: 42 g

Whole Roast Chicken

Prep Time: 5 Minutes
Cooking Time: 1 Hour
Servings: 4

Directions
1. Brush the chicken with olive oil using a brush. Mix the spices and sprinkle them over the chicken. If it is not enough to cover the whole chicken, add more spice mix.
2. Place the chicken in the fryer basket with the breast side down. Bake at 180°C for 45 minutes. Check once or twice that it is well cooked and not burnt.
3. After 45 minutes, turn the chicken so that the breast is facing upwards. Bake another 15 minutes.
4. Make sure the chicken is well cooked. You can pierce it with a sharp knife to see if the juices run clear. If it is not cooked, put it back in the fryer and heat it up some more, checking from time to time.

Nutrition: Calories: 390; Fat: 24 g; Carbohydrates: 1 g; Fibre: 0 g; Sugar: 0 g; Protein: 41 g

Ingredients
- 1 whole chicken (up to 2kg, depending on the size of your air fryer)
- 1tbsp olive oil
- 1tsp smoked paprika
- 1tsp dried mixed herbs
- 1tsp garlic granules/salt

Chicken Breasts with Spices

Prep Time: 10 Minutes
Cooking Time: 20 Minutes
Servings: 1

Ingredients
- 1 chicken breast (increase accordingly)
- 1/2 tbsp olive oil
- 1/2 tsp salt
- 1/2 tsp pepper
- 1/2 tsp garlic powder (or seasoning of your choice)

Directions
1. Preheat the air fryer to 180°C.
2. Grease or spray each chicken breast with oil. Season one side (smooth side) of the chicken breast.
3. Place the chicken breast (smooth side down) in the basket of the air fryer. Season the other side. Set the timer for 10 minutes. After 10 minutes, turn the chicken breast over so that it is cooked on both sides.
4. Check whether the chicken is fully cooked - use a meat thermometer if necessary. Allow the chicken to rest for 5 minutes before serving or slicing.

Nutrition: Calories: 266; Fat: 11 g; Carbohydrates: 2 g; Fibre: 0 g; Sugar: 0 g; Protein: 38 g

Chicken Thighs in Air Fryer

Prep Time: 5 Minutes
Cooking Time: 25 Minutes
Servings: 4-5

Directions
1. Preheat tyour air fryer to 200 °C. Lightly clean the chicken legs with kitchen paper before seasoning them.
2. Place the seasoned chicken legs in the air fryer. Depending on the size of your air fryer, you may have to do this in batches or use a trivet or rack if possible.
3. Cook for 10 minutes before turning the thighs over. Cook for a further 10 minutes. They should be crispy and fully cooked - if not, put them back in the air fryer for another 5 minutes or until cooked through. Internal temperature should be 75C.
4. Enjoy them with your favourite side dish!

Nutrition: Calories: 552; Fat: 41.5 g; Protein: 41 g; Carbs: 0 g; Fibre: 0 g; Sugar: 0 g

Ingredients
- 1 kg chicken thighs
- 2 tsp your Seasoning of choice (Piri Piri, Curry, Garlic, Chili etc...)

Chicken Drumsticks with Spices

Prep Time: 5 Minutes
Cooking Time: 25 Minutes
Servings: 4

Ingredients
- 8 - 12 chicken drumsticks
- Seasoning of choice (Piri Piri, Curry, Garlic, Chili etc...)
- Oil (optional)

Directions
1. Preheat the air fryer to 200°C for 5 minutes. You can brush the legs with oil if you desire. Season the chicken with your favorite spices. Feel free to add just salt if you like.
2. Place the drumsticks in the basket of the air fryer. You may need to use a trivet to fit them all. Or, if you're using a smaller air fryer, you'll have to cook in batches.
3. Air fry for 22-25 minutes, flipping halfway through. Make sure the chicken is fully cooked - inside it should reach 75°C. If possible, use a meat thermometer

Nutrition: Calories: 533; Fat: 28 g; Carbohydrates: 0 g; Fibre: 0 g; Sugar: 0 g; Protein: 66 g

Crispy Chicken Nuggets

Prep Time: 10 Minutes
Cooking Time: 8 Minutes
Servings: 4-5

Directions
1. Cut chicken breasts up into small chunks (nuggets size).
2. Melt the butter in the microwave. Place the breadcrumbs in a bowl. You can buy bread crumbs, or if you have a few slices of bread, you can do it by yourself breaking them into crumbs (you can pulse the bread to turn it into crumbs using a blender).
3. Then, first dip the chicken in the melted butter (or beaten eggs if using beaten eggs instead), then roll in the bread crumbs.
4. Repeat with each chicken chunks and then place them in your air fryer basket. Depending on the air fryer's size, you may need to cook in two batches.
5. Cook at 200°C for 8 minutes. Check to see if it's fully cooked before serving.

Nutrition: Calories: 555; Fat: 33 g; Protein: 48 g; Carbs: 12 g; Fibre: 0.5 g; Sugar: 1 g

Ingredients
- 3 to 4 boneless chicken breasts
- 4 tbsp butter or 3 to 4 beat eggs, (approx)
- 100 g breadcrumbs, (approx)
- seasoning or spices of your choice, salt, pepper, paprika etc

Chicken Parmesan in Air Fryer

Prep Time: 10 Mins
Cooking Time: 14 Mins
Servings: 4

Ingredients

- 2 large boneless chicken breasts
- Salt
- Freshly ground black pepper
- 40 g plain flour
- 2 large eggs
- 100 g panko bread crumbs
- 25 g freshly grated Parmesan
- 1 tsp. dried oregano
- 1/2 tsp. garlic powder
- 1/2 tsp. chilli flakes
- 240 g marinara/tomato sauce
- 100 g grated mozzarella
- Freshly chopped parsley, for garnish

Directions

1. Gently butterfly the chicken, cutting in half widthwise to obtain 4 thin chicken pieces. Season with salt and pepper on both sides.
2. Place the flour in a shallow bowl and season with a large pinch of salt and pepper. Put the eggs in a second bowl and beat them. In a third bowl, mix together the breadcrumbs, parmesan cheese, oregano, garlic powder, and chilli flakes.
3. Working with chicken pieces one at a time, coat them in flour, then dip them in the eggs and finally press them into the panko mixture, being careful to coat both sides well.
4. Working in batches as needed, place the chicken in the basket and air fry at 200°C for 5 minutes per side. Top chicken with sauce and mozzarella and cook at 200°C for a further 3 minutes or until cheese is melted and golden.
5. Garnish with parsley to serve.

Nutrition: Calories: 419.5; Fat: 16 g; Protein: 30 g; Carbs: 32 g; Fibre: 3 g; Sugar: 10 g

Chicken Kiev Balls in Air Fryer

Prep Time: 20 min
Cooking Time: 10 min
Servings: 12

Directions

1. Stir in butter, chopped parsley, and minced garlic. You can use a food processor, but don't process it for too long or will be too soft.
2. Divide the spiced butter into 12 equal parts. Place in the refrigerator (or freezer if time is short) to harden.
3. If you're already using a whole chicken breast instead of chopped/minced meat, you'll need to run it through a food processor or high-speed blender.
4. Once the garlic butter balls have hardened a little, it's time to work. Take a small piece of chicken at a time and wrap it in a thin layer of about 1-1.5cm around each ball of butter.
5. Place the eggs in a bowl and the breadcrumbs in another one and prepare the chicken balls for dipping. Season the crumbs to your liking (salt, pepper, paprika powder if you need a little more seasoning).
6. Dip the balls in the beaten eggs and roll them in the breadcrumbs. Make sure the crumbs are held tightly. Otherwise, the air fryer may blow the crumbs away. If necessary, press firmly by hand.
7. Spray them with oil (using an oil sprayer) and place them in an air fryer basket. Bake at 200°C for 10 minutes, and turn it over halfway through.

Ingredients
- 300 g chicken (breast or ground)
- 3 cloves garlic, crushed
- 100 g breadcrumbs
- 120 g butter
- 2 fresh parsley sprigs
- 2 eggs, beaten

Nutrition: Calories: 130; Fat: 9 g; Protein: 6 g; Carbs: 4 g; Fibre: 0 g; Sugar: 0.5 g

Turkey Burgers Easy Way

Prep Time: 5 Mins
Cooking Time: 15 Mins
Servings: 4

Ingredients

- 500 g ground lean turkey
- 1 large egg
- ½ tbsp cajun seasoning; substitute for poultry seasoning or any other seasoning of choice.
- ½ tbsp onion powder: substitute with cup of grated fresh onions or shallot.
- 2 tbsp fresh parsley chopped
- 1 Avocado pulp about cup
- Salt and pepper to taste
- Worcestershire sauce, optional use 1 tablespoon if using

Directions

1. In a medium bowl, gently mix together ground turkey, Cajun seasoning, egg, avocado, onion powder, parsley, and salt using your hands. Don't mix the ingredients too much to avoid the meat becoming tough. Shape the mixture into 4 to 6 equal sized patties, depending on how thick you want them, then place on a plate while you preheat the air fryer. (Wet your palm with water to facilitate the formation of the patties)
2. Preheat your air fryer to 180°C for 3 minutes. When the time is up, spray the basket with cooking oil and carefully place the burgers in.
3. Air fry the burgers for 15 to 20 minutes until well cooked through, depending on how thick they are. Flip the burgers halfway through cooking. Note: The internal temperature of a well-cooked turkey burger should be at least 75°C. Then the meat is safe to eat.
4. If you want to add toppings to the burgers, open the air fryer when the cooking cycle is complete and place the slices of cheese on the them, then allow the heat to melt the cheese.
5. Serve with salad or buns, as you like

Nutrition: Calories: 259.5; Fat: 15.5 g; Protein: 26.5 g; Carbs: 3 g; Fibre: 2 g; Sugar: 0 g

Garlic Herb Turkey Breast

Prep Time: 5 minutes
Cooking Time: 45 minutes
Servings: 6

Directions
1. Pat the turkey breast dry and add salt and pepper on both sides.
2. Take a small bowl, mix melted butter, garlic, thyme, and rosemary.
3. Brush the butter all over the turkey breast.
4. Arrange in your Air Fryer basket, skin side up, cook at 190ºC (170ºC fan), 40 minutes, until internal temperature reaches 73ºC, flip halfway through.
5. Let it rest for 5 minutes before slicing.

Nutrition: Calories: 328; Fat: 18 g; Protein: 33 g; Carbs: 5.5 g; Fibre: 0.5 g; Sugar: 0 g

Ingredients
- 900 g turkey breast, skin on
- Salt
- 1 tsp. freshly chopped rosemary
- Freshly ground black pepper
- 1 tsp. freshly chopped thyme
- 4 tbsp. butter, melted
- 3 cloves garlic, crushed

Simple Pork Chops

Prep Time: 5 Minutes
Cooking Time: 12 Minutes
Servings: 1

Ingredients
- 1 pork chop
- 1/2 tbsp olive oil
- 1/2 tbsp seasoning (BBQ, Curried, Garlic and Herb, Peri Peri etc...)

Directions
1. Preheat your air fryer to 200°C.
2. Brush both sides of the pork chop with oil. Add spices and massage evenly.
3. Place the pork chop in your air fryer and set timer for 12 minutes. Flip it after 6 minutes.
4. Make sure the pork chop is fully cooked. The outside should be golden brown and the juices should be clear.

Nutrition: Calories: 629; Fat: 45 g; Protein: 51 g; Carbs: 0 g; Fibre: 0 g; Sugar: 0 g

Steak in Air Fryer

Prep Time: 5 Minutes
Cooking Time: 8 Minutes
Servings: 1

Directions
1. Remove the steak from the refrigerator and leave it at room temperature for at least 30 minutes.
2. Preheat your air fryer to 200 °C. If desired, rub both sides of the steak with a little oil. Place the steak in the air fryer - on the trivet or directly on the bottom of the air fryer basket.
3. Set the timer to the desired time, depending on how well you want it cooked. Flip the steak halfway through. At the end of the cooking time, check to see if the steak is to your liking, remove it from the air fryer and let it rest for at least 5 minutes.

Nutrition: Calories: 331; Fat: 26 g; Carbohydrates: 0 g; Fibre: 0 g; Sugar: 0 g; Protein: 23 g

Ingredients
› Sirloin steak (or the cut you prefer)
› Oil (optional)
› Pepper and Salt

Easy Meatballs in Air Fryer

Prep Time: 10 Minutes
Cooking Time: 7 Minutes
Servings: 4

Ingredients
- 500g lean beef mince, (1 pound)
- 1 clove garlic, crushed
- 1 tsp dried mixed herbs
- 1 egg
- 1 tbsp breadcrumbs, (optional)

Directions
1. Mix all ingredients together until well blended. Form small round balls with your hands (this recipe makes about 16, depending on the size of the meatballs).
2. Place the meatballs in the air fryer and cook at 180°C for 7 minutes. Check halfway and turn over if necessary.
3. If you want to add sauce, place the meatballs in a ovenproof dish/pan after cooking. Pour the tomato sauce of your choice over the top and place in the airfryer tray. Air Fry at 180°C for about 6-8 minutes or until sauce is warm.
4. Serve with spaghetti and melted cheese (optional).

Nutrition: Calories: 267; Fat: 11 g; Carbohydrates: 2 g; Fibre: 0 g; Sugar: 0 g; Protein: 38 g

Beef Wellington

Prep Time: 15 minutes
Cooking Time: 35 minutes
Servings: 8

Directions
1. Season the beef with salt, pepper and wrap tightly in cling film
2. Place the beef in the refrigerator for at least one hour
3. Roll out the pastry and brush the edges with the beaten egg
4. Spread the pate over the pastry, making sure it is distributed equally
5. Take now the beef out of the refrigerator and remove the cling film
6. Place the beef in the middle of your pastry
7. Wrap your pastry around the meat and seal the edges with a fork
8. Place in the Air Fryer and cook at 160ºC for 35 minutes

Nutrition: Calories: 509; Fat: 28 g; Protein: 34 g; Carbs: 28 g; Fibre: 1 g; Sugar: 0.5 g

Ingredients
- 1kg beef fillet (one large piece)
- Chicken pate
- 2 sheets of shortcrust pastry
- 1 egg, beaten
- Salt
- Pepper

Simple Hamburgers

Prep Time: 5 minutes
Cooking Time: 15 minutes
Servings: 4

Ingredients
- 500 g minced beef
- Salt
- Pepper

Directions
1. Preheat Air Fryer to 200ºC.
2. Divide minced beef into 4 equal portions and form them into burgers with your hands.
3. Season with salt, pepper, to your taste.
4. Air fry for 10 minutes.
5. Flip your burgers over, cook for a further 3 minutes.

Nutrition: Calories: 247.5; Fat: 15 g; Protein: 24 g; Carbs: 0 g; Fibre: 0 g; Sugar: 0 g

Lamb Steaks

Prep Time: 5 minutes
Cooking Time: 10 minutes
Servings: 4

Directions
1. Place the lamb steaks on a chopping board, season with salt, pepper and dried thyme.
2. Thinly chop two tablespoons of mint and load into a bowl with everything except the lamb. Mix well then spoon over the lamb steaks. Place the steaks into the fridge for an hour, allow to marinate.
3. Place the steaks into the Air Fryer basket, add extra mint.
4. Air fry 10 minutes, 180°C.

Nutrition: Calories: 274.5; Fat: 19 g; Protein: 21g; Carbs: 4 g; Fibre: 0 g; Sugar: 4 g

Ingredients
- 4 Lamb Steaks
- 1 tsp. Frozen Chopped Garlic
- 2 tsp. Extra Virgin Olive Oil
- 2 tsp. Lemon Juice
- 2 tsp. Honey
- 1 tsp. Thyme
- Salt & Pepper
- Fresh Mint

Roast Beef in Air Fryer

Prep Time: 5 minutes
Cooking Time: 35 minutes
Servings: 8

Ingredients
- 1 Kg Beef Roast (up to 1.5 Kg)
- 1 tbsp Olive Oil
- Seasoning to taste

Directions
1. Tie the roast to make it more compact
2. Rub the roast with oil
3. Add any seasonings you like
4. Place the beef in the air fryer basket
5. Air fry at 180°C for about 15 minutes per half of Kg (for medium rare beef).
6. Let the roast rest for 5 minutes and serve

Notes
Rare: 46 to 49°C (50 final temperature)
Medium-Rare: 50 to 55°C (58 final temperature)
Medium: 58 to 60°C (63 final temperature)
Medium-Well: 60 to 63°F (65 final temperature)
Well-Done: 65 to 69°F (72 final temperature)

Nutrition: Calories: 443; Fat: 29 g; Carbohydrates: 0 g; Fiber: 0 g; Sugar: 0 g; Protein: 43 g;

Prawn Skewers with Tandoori

Prep Time: 9 mins
Cooking Time: 6 mins
Servings: 6

Directions
1. Cut the skewers according to the size of the pan or tray you will use.
2. Take a bowl and mix in yoghurt, tandoori masala, garlic and the juice of ½ a lemon.
3. use kitchen towels to dry the prawns.
4. Add all the prawns to the bowl and stir to coat.
5. Thread the prawns onto the kebab sticks.
6. Preheat to 200°C, spray with oil and air fry for about 8 minutes. No need to turn halfway through.

Nutrition: Calories: 58kcal; Carbohydrates: 4g; Protein: 8g; Fat: 1g; Fibre: 1g; Sugar: 1g

Equipment
- Wooden Kebab Sticks

Ingredients
- Spray oil
- 300 grams King Prawn

Tandoori Marinade:
- 3 tbsp Fat Free Yoghurt Can use full fat instead
- 2 tbsp Tandoori Masala Spice Blend Powder
- 2 cloves Garlic Crushed
- 1 Lemon ½ for the juice, ½ sliced into wedges to serve

Optional:
- 1 tbsp Chopped Coriander to sprinkle on top of chicken after cooking

Ingredients

For the base:
- 300g minced beef
- 4 tbsp onions (coarsely diced)
- 2 tbsp carrots (coarsely diced)
- 4 mushrooms (soaked & diced)
- 4 cloves garlic (minced)
- 1 tsp dried mixed herbs
- 2 bay leaves
- 150 ml beef stock
- 1 tbsp Bovril
- 1 tsp ground black pepper
- 2 tbsp plain flour
- 30g butter

For the potato topping:
- 400g potatoes (quartered)
- 130 ml milk
- 2 tbsp butter
- Pinch of salt

Final egg wash topping:
- 1 egg yolk (beaten)

Cottage Pie

Prep Time: 15 minutes
Cooking Time: 40 minutes
Servings: 4

Directions

1. Add 1 teaspoon of salt to a saucepan of water and bring to a boil before adding the potatoes. Cook the potatoes until very tender(15-17 minutes).
2. Melt the butter on the baking tray while preheating the fryer. Everything is prepared on the baking tray at 180 degrees C for this recipe.
3. Fry the onion for 1 minute, then add the garlic and fry for another minute until fragrant.
4. Add the ground beef, carrots, mushrooms, herb mix, black pepper, and bay leaves, mix well and cook for 20 minutes. Stir well every 5 minutes.
5. After 10 minutes, add Bovril and beef broth and stir. Continue stirring every 5 minutes.
6. Sprinkle all-purpose flour into the mixture and mix well 2-3 minutes before the end of the cooking time.
7. Hold the baking tray in the air fryer (to keep it warm) while you mash the potatoes.
8. Add the butter, salt, and milk (a little at a time) to the potatoes, mash, and mix well.
9. Spread mashed potatoes over the meat mixture, leveling with the back of a spoon.
10. Use a fork to draw lines across mashed potatoes, then pour the egg yolk on top.
11. Return the baking tray to the air fryer and cook at 180°C for 20 minutes.
12. Serve warm

Nutrition: Calories 360; Fat 22 g; Protein 19 g; Carbs 20 g; Fiber 2.5 g; Sugar 3 g

Salmon Fillet in Air Fryer

Prep Time: 5 Minutes
Cooking Time: 10 Minutes
Servings: 2

Ingredients
- 2 salmon fillets
- 1/2 tbsp olive oil
- Salt and pepper to season

Directions
1. Turn on your air fryer and set the temperature to 200°C.
2. Brush each salmon fillet with a little oil and season with salt and pepper or your favorite seasoning/marinade.
3. Lightly spray the airfryer basket with oil and place the salmon fillets in the basket. Air Fry for 8 minutes. At this point, check to see if they are done. Heat for an additional 1-2 minutes, if necessary.

Nutrition: Calories: 310.5; Fat: 15.5 g; Protein: 39 g; Carbs: 0 g; Fibre: 0 g; Sugar: 0 g

Garlic and Butter Shrimps

Prep Time: 10 Mins
Cooking Time: 8 Mins
Servings: 4

Directions

1. Clean the shrimps: devein them and remove the shell, if desired. Transfer the shrimp to an ovenproof dish that fits in your air fryer basket.
2. Season the shrimp with salt, pepper, garlic, drizzle with a little cooking oil and toss to combine. Add cubes of butter to the shrimp, then place in the fry basket.
3. Fry at 200°C for 8 to 10 minutes. There's no need to flip the shrimp, but you can do it just in case.
4. Remove from the fryer, add some chopped parsley and squeeze some lemon juice over the shrimp if desired. Stir to combine. Serve and enjoy!

Nutrition: Calories: 169 kcal; Carbohydrates: 1 g; Protein: 23 g; Fat: 8 g; Fibre: 1 g; Sugar: 1 g

Ingredients

- 450 g shrimps: frozen, thawed or fresh
- 1 large fresh garlic clove minced (or garlic powder)
- 30 g unsalted butter cut into small cubes
- Salt and pepper to taste
- cooking oil spay (you can also do without it)
- ½ lemon juice
- 1 tbsp parsley chopped to garnish

Cod with Butter and Lemon

Prep Time: 5 Mins
Cooking Time: 10 Mins
Servings: 4

Ingredients
- 4 (125g each) Fresh Cod loins (or fillets as you like)
- 30 g melted unsalted butter
- 1 Lemon sliced
- Salt to taste
- black pepper to taste

Directions
1. Preheat the fryer to 200°C for 5 minutes.
2. Dry the cod fillets. Season the fish generously with salt and black pepper, then brush with the melted butter (just on one side of the fish)
3. Spray the frying basket with cooking oil. Place the cod fillets/loins in the basket, buttered side down, taking care that they do not touch each other. Brush the remaining butter over the fish, add a lemon slice to each fillet.
4. Cook for 10 minutes, carefully remove the fish and place on a plate.
5. Serve with lemon butter sauce, roast potatoes and vegetables and enjoy!

Nutrition: Calories: 85 kcal; Carbohydrates: 3 g; Protein: 1 g; Fat: 6 g; Fibre: 1 g; Sugar: 1 g

Crab Cakes with Tartar Sauce

Prep Time: 15 Mins
Cooking Time: 15 Mins
Servings: 4

Directions
1. Prepare crab cakes: In a large bowl, whisk together the mayonnaise, egg, scallions, Dijon mustard, Cajun seasoning, lemon zest, and salt. Add crab meat and cracker crumbs.
2. Distribute the mixture evenly and shape into 8 patties. You can keep them in the fridge for up to 4 hours if you don't want to fry them yet. (They can also be frozen on a parchment-lined baking tray.)
3. Heat your air fryer to 190°C and spray the basket and the crab cakes with cooking spray. Arrange crab cakes in the basket in a single layer. Air fry until golden and crispy, about 12-14 minutes, turning halfway through.
4. In the meantime, prepare the tartar sauce: Mix all the ingredients for the sauce in a bowl.
5. Serve the crab cakes warm with the hot sauce (optional), lemon wedges and tartar sauce.

Nutrition: Calories: 320; Fat: 14 g; Protein: 25 g; Carbs: 19.5 g; Fibre: 2 g; Sugar: 0.25 g

Ingredients
For The Crab Cakes
- 60 g mayonnaise
- 1 egg
- 2 tbsp. chives, finely chopped
- 2 tsp. Dijon mustard
- 2 tsp. cajun seasoning
- 1 tsp. lemon zest
- 1/2 tsp. salt
- 450 g jumbo lump crab meat
- 120 g Cracker crumbs (from about 20 crackers)
- Cooking spray
- Hot sauce, for serving
- Lemon wedges, for serving

For The Tartar Sauce
- 60 g mayonnaise
- 80.5 g dill pickle, finely chopped
- 1 tbsp. shallot, finely chopped
- 2 tsp. capers, finely chopped
- 1 tsp. fresh lemon juice
- 1/4 tsp. Dijon mustard
- 1 tsp. fresh dill, finely chopped

Coconut Prawns with Sauce

Prep Time: 5 Mins
Cooking Time: 12 Mins
Servings: 4

Ingredients

For The Prawns
- 65 g plain flour
- Salt
- Freshly ground black pepper
- 100 g panko bread crumbs
- 35 g shredded sweetened coconut
- 2 large eggs, beaten
- 450 g large prawns, peeled and deveined, tails on

For The Dipping Sauce
- 120 g mayonnaise
- 1 tbsp. Sriracha
- 1 tbsp. Thai sweet chilli sauce

Directions

1. In a shallow bowl, season the flour with salt and pepper. In another shallow bowl, mix the breadcrumbs and coconut. Place the eggs in a third shallow bowl.
2. Dip the prawns one by one in flour, then in eggs, then in coconut mixture.
3. Put the prawns in the frying basket and air fry to 200°C.
4. Cook until they are golden brown and cooked through, 10 to 12 minutes. Work in batches as needed.
5. In a small bowl, mix together the mayonnaise, sriracha, and chilli sauce. Serve prawns with the sauce.

Nutrition: Calories: 374; Fat: 16.5 g; Protein: 29 g; Carbs: 25 g; Fibre: 3 g; Sugar: 2 g

Fish and Chips

Prep Time: 8 mins
Cooking Time: 12 mins
Servings: 2

Directions

1. Preheat air fryer to 200 C, air fryer setting. In a medium bowl, whisk together half the flour, cornstarch, baking soda, beer or water, and egg until smooth. Set aside.
2. Whisk together the remaining flour, salt, black pepper, paprika, and garlic powder in another medium bowl.
3. Dip the cod, piece by piece, into the batter. Drain excess and coat in the flour mixture. Spray the air fryer basket well with cooking spray or use a piece of parchment paper. Place the fish in the basket, ensuring the pieces don't touch each other.
4. Spray the fish too with a little of cooking spray.
5. Air fry for 10 to 12 minutes at 200 C. Halfway through cooking, spray again with more cooking spray. Turning is not necessary. It's ready when the fish is golden.
6. Sprinkle with a bit of salt if you like.
7. Arrange, serve and enjoy! You can serve with French fries, lemon wedges and tartar sauce for dipping.

Nutrition: Calories 417; Fat 4 g; Carbohydrates 52 g; Protein 40 g; Fibre 2 g; Sugar 1 g

Ingredients

- 130 g all-purpose flour, divided
- 1 tbsp cornstarch
- 1/4 tsp baking soda
- 80 ml room temperature beer or water
- 1 egg
- 1/2 tsp salt
- 1/2 tsp black pepper
- 1/2 tsp paprika
- 1/4 tsp garlic powder
- 340 g cod filets, thawed
- Cooking spray

Tuna Patties

Prep time: 15 minutes
Cooking Time: 10 minutes
Servings: 10

Ingredients
- 425 g canned albacore tuna, drained or 454g fresh tuna, diced
- 2-3 large eggs
- zest of 1 medium lemon
- 1 tbsp. lemon juice
- 1/4 tsp of Kosher salt, or to taste
- 55 g of bread crumbs
- 1/2 tsp dried herbs (oregano, dill, basil, thyme or any combo)
- fresh cracked black pepper
- 3 tbsp grated parmesan cheese
- 1 stalk celery, finely chopped

Optional: tarter sauce, ranch, mayo, lemon slices
- 3 tbsp minced onion
- 1/2 tsp garlic powder

Directions
1. Take a medium bowl, mix the lemon zest, eggs, lemon juice, bread crumbs, celery, parmesan cheese, onion, dried herbs, garlic powder, salt, pepper. Now stir well. Gently fold in the tuna.
2. Take your Air Fryer perforated baking paper, lay it inside the base of the Air Fryer. Now lightly spray the paper. if not you don't have it spray at the base of the Air Fryer basket to make sure they do not stick.
3. Try to keep all patties same size and thickness. Scoop 1/4 cup of the mixture, shape into patties about 8 cm wide x 1.3 cm thick and lay them inside the basket. Makes about 10 patties.
4. If patties are too soft, chill them for 1 hour or until firm. Brush the top of the patties with oil. Air Fry 185°C, 10 minutes, flip halfway through. After you flip the patties, spray the tops again.
5. Serve with your sauce and lemon slices.

Nutrition: Calories: 102.2; Fat: 3.9 g; Protein: 12.5 g; Carbs: 2.7 g; Fibre: 0 g; Sugar: 0 g

2 Ingredient Air Fryer Pizza

Prep time: 5 Minutes
Cooking Time: 10 Minutes
Servings: 2

Directions
1. Mix the self-rising flour and yogurt until you get a dough consistency (add more flour if needed). Divide the dough into two. Roll each one out on a floured surface.
2. Place a parchment paper in the basket of your air-fryer and air fry at 200°C for 8-10 minutes, turning halfway through.
3. Remove the pizza and top with your favourite toppings such as pizza sauce or shredded cheese.
4. Return to airfryer basket and cook for 3 more minutes. Repeat with the second pizza.

Nutrition: Calories: 665.5; Fat: 4 g; Protein: 35 g; Carbs: 129.5 g; Fibre: 18.5 g; Sugar: 4 g

Ingredients
- 240 g natural or Greek yoghurt
- 350 g self-raising flour
- grated cheese (enough to sprinkle on 2 small pizzas)
- pizza sauce/passata
- toppings of your choice (pepperoni, pineapple, peppers, chicken etc)

Pizza Rolls Recipe

Prep time: 10 Minutes
Cooking Time: 8 Minutes
Servings: 4

Ingredients
- 240 g natural/Greek yoghurt
- 350 g self raising flour
- 1 tin/carton of passata/pizza sauce (or enough to cover the dough)
- Grated cheese (Mozzarello or your favourite one)
- 1 tsp dried herbs (optional)

Directions
1. Make the dough by mixing flour and yogurt in a bowl. If the mixture is too wet and sticky, add a little more flour. Add more water if it's too dry. You should be able to stretch the dough without it sticking or falling off.
2. Roll out the dough into a rectangle on a lightly floured surface. Spread the pizza sauce/passata on the dough. You can use your favorite pizza sauce or regular pasta sauce. But be careful not to make it too watery. Otherwise, it will run off the dough.
3. Sprinkle grated cheese over tomato sauce and add your favorite toppings. Carefully roll the pizza lengthwise until it forms a sausage shape. Using a sharp or serrated knife, cut pizza roll into even slices.
4. Carefully place the rolls into the airfryer basket. Air Fry at 180 °C for about 8 to12 minutes. Check halfway through to make sure it's cooking too quickly.

Nutrition: Calories: 393; Fat: 5 g; Carbohydrates: 72 g; Fibre: 3 g; Sugar: 6 g; Protein: 14 g

Chimichanga

Prep time: 15 Mins
Cooking Time: 50 Mins
Servings: 8

Directions

1. In a medium-sized skillet, heat the oil over medium heat. Add onions and cook until tender, about 5 minutes.
2. Add the garlic, chilli powder, cumin and garlic powder. Cook until fragrant, about 1 minute.
3. Add sauce and simmer, then add shredded chicken and toss to coat.
4. Season with salt and pepper then remove from the heat.
5. Distribute about 65g of beans in the middle of the tortilla and then sprinkle with both cheeses. Garnish with approx. 70 g chicken mixture and some sour cream.
6. Roll into a burrito by folding the top and bottom of the tortilla in half, then folding the right side completely over the filling, tucking in and rolling up tightly.
7. Place seam-side down on a plate and repeat with the remaining tortillas and filling.
8. Working in batches as needed, place the burritos seam-side down in the air fryer basket and spray with some cooking spray. Air fry for 5 minutes at 200°C, then turn, spray with more cooking spray and cook for another 5 minutes.
9. Drizzle with more sour cream and serve with guacamole.

Ingredients

- Cooking spray
- 1 tbsp. extra-virgin olive oil
- 1 small yellow onion, chopped
- 2 cloves garlic, crushed
- 1 tsp. chilli powder
- 1 tsp. ground cumin
- 1/2 tsp. garlic powder
- 190 g salsa
- 550 g shredded cooked chicken
- Ground black pepper and Salt
- 1 x 400g can refried beans
- 8 large flour tortillas
- 80 g grated cheddar
- 80 g grated pepper jack cheese
- 120 g sour cream, plus more for serving
- Guacamole, for serving

Nutrition: Calories: 318.5; Fat: 20.5 g; Protein: 21 g; Carbs: 12 g; Fibre: 0.5 g; Sugar: 3 g

Falafel in Air Fryer

Prep time: 10 Mins
Cooking Time: 15 Mins
Servings: 20

Ingredients

For Falafel
- 1/2 medium yellow onion, cut into quarters
- 4 cloves garlic
- 5 g packed parlsey leaves
- 5 g packed coriander leaves
- 2 x 400g cans chickpeas, rinsed and drained
- 1 tsp. salt
- 1 tsp. baking powder
- 1 tsp. dried coriander
- 1/2 tsp. chilli flakes

For Tahini Sauce
- 80 g tahini
- Juice of 1/2 a lemon
- 3 tbsp. water, plus more as needed
- Pinch of salt
- Pinch of chilli flakes

Directions

1. In a food processor, puree the onion, garlic, parsley and cilantro until finely chopped, scraping the sides as needed. Add drained chickpeas, salt, baking powder, coriander, cumin and chili flakes. Pulse again until most of the chickpeas have broken down into a few pieces. Stop just before the mixture turns into a paste. Taste and adjust seasonings to your liking.
2. Scoop out about 2 tablespoons of the mixture and gently form a ball without pressing too hard or the falafel will be dense.
3. Put the falafel in the frying basket and air fry for 15 minutes at 190 °C.
4. Meanwhile, make the tahini sauce: In a medium bowl, combine the tahini and lemon juice. Add water and stir until combined. Add water, 1 tablespoon at a time, until desired consistency is reached.
5. Season with a large pinch of salt and chilli flakes. Serve falafel as is with sauce, on a salad or in a pita.

Nutrition: Calories: 374; Fat: 16.5 g; Protein: 29 g; Carbs: 25 g; Fibre: 3 g; Sugar: 2 g

Chapter 3
SIDE DISH RECIPES

Yorkshire Puddings

Prep Time: 1 hour
Cooking Time: 18 minutes
Servings: 4

Ingredients
- 1 egg
- 4 tbsp (70 g) flour
- 4 tbsp (80 ml) milk
- 4 tbsp (80 ml) water
- 1/4 tsp salt

Directions
1. Mix well all the ingredients together; you need to obtain a smooth batter with no lumps
2. Once the batter is ready, refrigerate for 30 to 60 minutes
3. Preheat the air fryer to 200 C
4. Grease a ramekin with some butter, then add a tsp of oil; heat at 200C in the air fryer for five minutes. This operation will prevent the batter from sticking
5. Once the ramekins are hot, add five tablespoons of Yorkshire Pudding mixture to each one
6. Cook at 200 C for 18 minutes
7. Do not open the air fryer while cooking!

Nutrition: Calories 89; Fat 2 g; Protein 4 g; Carbs 13 g; Fibre 2 g; Sugar 1 g

Roast Potatoes in Air Fryer

Prep Time: 10 mins
Cooking Time: 30 mins
Servings: 4

Directions
1. Wash the potatoes with water and after peeling, cut them into quarters
2. Put the potatoes in a pot of cold water and bring to the boil. Once the water boils, cook for 4 minutes.
3. Meanwhile, preheat the air fryer to 200°C
4. Drain in colander and bash around a little to rough up the edges
5. Place in a bowl, add oil and black pepper (do not add salt yet)
6. Add potatoes to the air fryer. Cook for 25 minutes at 200°C.
7. Turn ½ way through cooking time
8. Season with salt and pepper after cooking.

Nutrition: Calories: 193kcal; Carbohydrates: 44g; Protein: 5g; Fat: 1g; Fibre: 6g; Sugar: 2g

Ingredients
- 1 kg White Potatoes Maris Piper or King Edwards
- 2 tbsp Vegetable Oil
- black pepper
- salt

Chunky Chips in Air Fryer

Prep Time: 12 mins
Cooking Time: 33 mins
Servings: 2

Ingredients
- 4 Medium Potatoes Maris Piper or King Edwards
- 1 tbsp Rapeseed Oil or Canola / Vegetable / Olive Oil
- Salt to taste
- Pepper to taste

Directions
1. Peel the potatoes - this is optional and can be cooked with the skins on. Cut the potato lengthwise into 2-3 pieces (depending on the size of the potato!)
2. Rinse or soak in cold water to remove starch.
3. Put the potatoes in a pot and pour cold water into it and bring to boil. After boiling for 5-7 minutes they should be soft enough to pierce with a fork. Do not overheat or they will fall apart.
4. Place the boiled potatoes on a wire rack using a slotted spoon. Allow to air dry while preheating the air fryer.
5. Preheat air fryer to 200°C
6. Brush them with oil.
7. Place in the air fryer and air fry for 15-20 minutes
8. Add your desired amount of salt and pepper.
9. Serve!

Nutrition: Calories: 62kcal; Fat: 7g

Spicy Curried Potato Wedges

Prep Time: 10 mins
Cooking Time: 35 mins
Servings: 6

Directions
1. First wash the whole potatoes. Cut the potatoes in half (1/2), cut each half in half (¼), cut each quarter in half (⅛), make 4 wedges. Repeat with the other half to make 8 wedges. Proceed in the same way with the remaining potatoes for a total of 24 wedges.
2. In a large bowl or ziplock bag, combine curry powder, garlic, salt, pepper and olive oil.
3. Add the potatoes, mix and coat.
4. Place in the air fryer, leaving space between each potato so that it cooks evenly. Cook for 15-20 minutes, turning the cloves halfway through cooking.

Nutrition: Calories: 122kcal; Carbohydrates: 13g; Protein: 2g; Fat: 7g; Fibre: 1g; Sugar: 1g

Ingredients
- 3 Medium-Large Potatoes about 470 g
- 1 tsp Curry Powder
- 2 Garlic Cloves crushed (1 teaspoon of Garlic Puree)
- 1/2 tsp each of Salt & Pepper
- 2 tbsp Olive Oil

Marinated Tofu

Prep Time: 10 Minutes
Cooking Time: 10 Minutes
Servings: 4

Ingredients
- 300 g firm tofu
- 2 tbsp soy sauce
- 2 tsp sesame oil
- 2 tsp seasoning of your choice (BBQ, Cajun, Curry, Garlic and Paprika)
- 2 tbsp cornflour

Directions
1. Using a sharp knife or kitchen scissors, cut the tofu into 2.5 cm cubes.
2. Place in a bowl and add the remaining ingredients and stir until the tofu is well seasoned.
3. Let the tofu marinate for 5 to 10 minutes. During this time you can preheat the fryer to 200°C.
4. Place the marinated tofu in the air fryer basket and cook for 10 minutes. After 5 minutes, shake the basket to ensure the tofu is crispy throughout.
5. Enjoy alone or with your favourite dip.

Nutrition: Calories: 88; Fat: 6 g; Carbohydrates: 2 g; Fibre: 1 g; Sugar: 1 g; Protein: 8 g

Broccoli in Air Fryer

Prep Time: 10 Mins
Cooking Time: 10 Mins
Servings: 2

Directions
1. Pour water into a kettle and bring to the boil (this step is optional only if you prefer to blanch the broccoli)
2. Cut the broccoli into florets (keep them if possible the same size) and put them in a bowl. Submerge the broccoli with the boiling water and let stand for about 30 seconds. Gently drain the broccoli and hold it under cold running water to prevent it from cooking.
3. Pat the broccoli dry with a kitchen towel or allow to cool slightly and air dry slightly if you are running out of time
4. In a bowl, place the vegetables and season with the garlic powder, lemon juice, honey, red pepper flakes, salt, black pepper, and olive oil, and toss to combine.
5. Place the vegetables in your air fryer basket (no need to spray the basket with oil) and cook at 180°C for 6 to 10 minutes, shaking the basket halfway to achieve even cooking. Serve immediately with a main meal of your choice.

Ingredients
- 1 head of broccoli
- 1 tbsp lemon juice
- 1 tbsp olive oil
- ½ tbsp honey Sub with maple syrup
- ½ tsp garlic powder
- ½ tsp red pepper flakes optional
- Salt to taste

Frozen broccoli
1. If you are using frozen broccoli, place them in the Air fryer basket and cook for 1 to 2 minutes until the vegetables are thawed. Sprinkle seasonings over the vegetables and mix, drizzle with cooking oil, toss and drizzle again to coat well.
2. Cook at 190°C for 10 to 15 minutes until the edges are crispy. Serve and enjoy!

Nutrition: Calories: 185 kcal; Carbohydrates: 26 g; Protein: 9 g; Fat: 8 g; Fibre: 8 g; Sugar: 10 g

Carrots with Simple Seasoning

Prep Time: 15 Mins
Cooking Time: 18 Mins
Servings: 4

Ingredients
- 1 kg carrots
- 1 tbsp olive oil
- ½ tsp red pepper flakes
- Salt and pepper to taste.
- Chopped parsley to garnish

Directions
1. Peel the carrots, trim both ends and cut diagonally into about 1.5 cm thick slices, then place in a bowl or oven-safe dish, if desired.
2. Season the carrots with salt, pepper, pepper flakes and olive oil, then toss.
3. Preheat the air fryer to 180°C for 3 minutes.
4. Place the carrots in the Air fryer basket and spread in a single layer. If you are using an oven-safe dish, place it directly in the basket of the Air fryer.
5. Air Fry the carrots, shaking the air fryer basket halfway, for 15 to 20 minutes until tender and caramelized on the edges.
6. Garnish with chopped parsley and a squeeze of lemon juice before serving.

Nutrition: Calories: 134 kcal; Carbohydrates: 24 g; Protein: 2 g; Fat: 4 g; Fibre: 7 g; Sugar: 12 g

Vegetables Roasted in Air Fryer

Prep Time: 10 Mins
Cooking Time: 12 Mins
Servings: 4

Directions

1. Wash the vegetables, remove the seeds from the peppers and chop the remaining vegetables into equal-sized pieces.
2. Place in a large bowl, then sprinkle with the smoked paprika, granulated garlic and herbs de Provence, salt and pepper, olive oil and lemon juice and mix. Marinate for 15 to 30 minutes (this step is optional)
3. Preheat you air fryer to 200°C for 3 minutes.
4. Place the vegetables in the basket and distribute well. Air Fry
5. for 10 to 15 minutes, shaking the basket every 4 to 5 minutes, until crispy and tender.
6. Serve and enjoy!

Nutrition: Calories: 158 kcal; Carbohydrates: 19 g; Protein: 6 g; Fat: 8 g; Fibre: 7 g; Sugar: 8 g

Ingredients
- 1 Zucchini/courgette
- 2 Bell peppers (can combine red and yellow bell pepper)
- 1 small head broccoli
- 1 medium red onion

Marinade
- 1 tsp Smoked paprika
- 1 tsp garlic granules
- 1 tsp Herb de provence
- Salt and pepper
- 1½ tbsp olive oil
- 2 tbsp Lemon juice

Frozen Mozzarella Sticks

Prep Time: 0 Mins
Cooking Time: 6 Mins
Servings: 24 Mozzarella Sticks

Ingredients

- 24 Frozen mozzarella sticks or bites this can be any brand of choice

Directions

1. Preheat your air fryer at 180C for 3 minutes.
2. Remove the frozen mozzarella sticks from its packaging and carefully arrange them in the basket in a single layer making sure to leave enough space between them
3. Cook at 180C for 6 minutes or until crispy on the outside and cheese melted in the middle.
4. Serve immediately with marinara dipping sauce or pizza sauce. enjoy!

Nutrition: Calories: 45 kcal; Protein: 6 g; Fat: 2 g

Chickpeas Simple Recipe

Prep Time: 5 Mins
Cooking Time: 13 Mins
Servings: 4

Directions
1. Preheat your air fryer to 190ºC for 3 minutes
2. Open the chickpeas can, drain in a colander and rinse under cold running water. Make sure the chickpeas are fully drained or alternatively, pat them dry with a kitchen towel or paper towel.
3. In a bowl, combine the chickpeas, smoked paprika, onion powder, cayenne pepper, salt, olive oil and mix
4. Pour the seasoned chickpeas into the air fryer basket and distribute. Cook at 190C for 12 to 15 minutes, stirring every 5 minutes, or until crispy to your taste.
5. Let cool for about 5 minutes and serve.

Nutrition: Calories: 128 kcal; Carbohydrates: 15 g; Protein: 5 g; Fat: 6 g; Fibre: 5 g; Sugar: 1 g

Ingredients
- 1 400 g Canned chickpeas
- 1 teaspoon smoked paprika or as needed
- ½ teaspoon onion powder
- ¼ teaspoon Cayenne pepper
- 1 Tablespoon Olive oil

Aubergine with Spices

Prep Time: 5 Mins
Cooking Time: 15 Mins
Servings: 4

Ingredients
- 1 medium aubergine
- 1 tbsp. extra-virgin olive oil
- 1 tsp. dried oregano
- 1/2 tsp. garlic powder
- Salt
- Freshly ground black pepper
- Pinch chilli flakes

Directions
1. Cut the ends of the aubergine and cut in half lengthwise. Cut each half into strips about 2.5 cm thick and 7 cm long.
2. In a medium bowl, add the eggplant, oil, and spices, tossing to coat.
3. Work in batches and arrange them in a single layer in the air fryer basket.
4. Air fry at 190°C for about 14 minutes until golden brown, shaking the basket once halfway through

Nutrition: Calories: 58; Fat: 3 g; Protein: 1 g; Carbs: 6.5 g; Fibre: 3 g; Sugar: 4 g

Cauliflower in Air Fryer

Prep Time: 5 Mins
Cooking Time: 12 Mins
Servings: 2-3

Directions
1. In a small bowl, mix the ghee, garlic powder, and turmeric.
2. In a large bowl, place the cauliflower and pour over the ghee mixture, stirring until all the florets are yellow. Season generously with salt and pepper.
3. Preheat your air fryer to 190°C for three minutes.
4. Place the cauliflower in a single layer in the basket and air fry, stirring, for 10-12 minutes halfway through cooking until golden brown.

Nutrition: Calories: 114; Fat: 11.5 g; Protein: 1 g; Carbs: 2.5 g; Fibre: 1 g; Sugar: 1 g

Ingredients
- 2 tbsp. ghee or butter, melted
- 1/2 tsp. garlic powder
- 1/4 tsp. turmeric
- 1 small head of cauliflower cut into small florets
- Salt
- Freshly ground black pepper

Courgette with Panko

Prep Time: 10 mins
Cooking Time: 18 mins
Servings: 4

Ingredients

- 2 medium courgette, sliced into ½ cm rounds
- 2 large eggs
- 90 g panko bread crumbs
- 50 g cornmeal
- 35 g freshly grated Parmesan
- 1 tsp. dried oregano
- 1/4 tsp. garlic powder
- Pinch chilli flakes
- Salt
- Freshly ground black pepper
- Marinara, for serving

Directions

1. Place the sliced courgettes on a plate lined with paper towels and pat dry.
2. Place the beaten eggs in a shallow bowl. In another shallow bowl, mix together the panko, cornmeal, parmesan cheese, oregano, garlic powder, and a large pinch of chilli flakes.
3. Season with salt and pepper.
4. One at a time, dipp the drained courgettes in the beaten egg, then in panko mixture, coating well.
5. Working in batches as needed, spread the courgettes in an even layer and cook at 200°C for 18 minutes, turning halfway through. Serve warm with marinara, if desired.

Nutrition: Calories: 192; Fat: 5.5 g; Protein: 8 g; Carbs: 24 g; Fibre: 2 g; Sugar: 2.5 g

Creamy Mashed Potatoes

Prep Time: 5 minutes
Cooking Time: 25 minutes
Servings: 4

Directions
1. Start by placing your potatoes into a foil packet, Layout your foil, then place the potatoes in them.
2. Air fry for 25 minutes at 200C. Check after 25 minutes if they are soft; The actual time will depend on the type of air fryer you have and the size of the potatoes.
3. Use a fork (or a potato masher if you prefer) to mash the potatoes.
4. Put the potatoes in a bowl.
5. Add the cream cheese and butter.
6. Add the chives and continue to mix. Continue mixing until the potatoes are mashed and the cream cheese and butter are combined.
7. Plate, serve and enjoy!

Nutrition: Calories: 322; Sugar: 3 g; Fat: 11 g; Carbohydrates: 50 g; Fibre: 5 g; Protein: 7 g

Ingredients
- 900 baking potatoes (small to medium)
- 40 g butter
- 60 g cream cheese
- 2 stalks of fresh chives
- salt and pepper to taste

Mashed Potato Pancakes

Prep Time: 5 minutes
Cooking Time: 15 minutes
Servings: 6

Ingredients
- 250 g Mashed Potatoes
- 100 g cheddar cheese
- 1 green onion chopped
- 2 strips of cooked bacon
- 1 egg
- 2 tbsp flour
- 100 g panko bread crumbs
- Salt and Pepper to taste

Directions
1. Mix Potatoes, egg, cheese, bacon, green onion, and flour
2. Make into a patty form.
3. Coat in panko bread crumbs
4. Place in the freezer for 10 minutes to hold form.
5. Place foil over your rack on your air fryer
6. Cook on 200 C for 10 minutes
7. Flip over and cook for an additional 5 minutes.

Nutrition: Calories: 273; Total Fat: 13g; Carbohydrates: 28g; Fibre: 2g; Sugar: 2g; Protein: 11g

Chapter 4

DESSERTS

Apple Crumble in Air Fryer

Prep Time: 10 mins
Cooking Time: 18 mins
Servings: 4-5

Ingredients
- 2 large Bramley apples
- 225 g plain flour
- 115 g butter
- 80 g Sugar

Directions
1. Preheat air fryer to 180°C.
2. Peel the apples, cut them into small pieces, and place them on a baking tin suitable for the air fryer. Combine flour and butter in a mixing bowl. Rub it with your hands until it looks like crumbs. Stir in sugar. Place the crumble mixture on top of the apples.
3. Place in air fryer basket for 18 minutes. After 15 minutes, check to see if it isn't cooking too quickly. When the crumble is golden brown, it's done.

Notes: Tastes great with custard or ice cream.

Nutrition: Calories: 388; Fat: 18 g; Protein: 5 g; Carbs: 52 g; Fibre: 5 g; Sugar: 19 g

Apricot and Raisin Cake

Prep Time: 10 Minutes
Cooking Time: 12 Minutes
Servings: 8

Directions
1. Preheat air fryer to 160°C
2. In a blender or food processor, puree the dried apricots and juices until smooth.
3. Put sugar and cake flour in another bowl and mix. Add a beaten egg to flour and sugar and mix together. Add apricot puree and raisins and keep mixing.
4. Spray a small amount of oil on a baking pan suitable for the air fryers. Transfer and flatten the mixture in it.
5. Cook in the air fryer for 12 minutes and check after 10 minutes. Use a metal skewer to check if it is done. If desired, return the cake to the air fryer and brown for a few more minutes.
6. Allow to cool, then remove from pan and slice.

Nutrition: Calories: 116; Fat: 1 g; Carbohydrates: 26 g; Fibre: 1 g; Sugar: 16 g; Protein: 2 g

Ingredients
- 75g dried apricots, (just under 1/2 cup)
- 4 tbsp orange juice
- 75g self-raising flour, (3/4 cup)
- 40 g Sugar, (1/3 cup)
- 1 egg
- 75g Raisins, (just under 1/2 a cup)

Carrot Cake in Air Fryer

Prep Time: 10 Minutes
Cooking Time: 25 Minutes
Servings: 5-6

Ingredients
- 140 g Soft brown sugar
- 2 eggs, beaten
- 140 g butter
- 1 orange, zest & juice
- 200 g self-raising flour
- 1 tsp ground cinnamon
- 175 g grated carrot, (approx 2 medium carrots)
- 60 g sultanas

Directions
1. Preheat the fryer to 175°C.
2. In a bowl, mix the butter and sugar.
3. Gradually add the beaten eggs
4. Gradually add the flour while stirring. Add orange juice and zest, grated carrots and sultanas.
5. Gently mix all the ingredients.
6. Grease the baking pan and pour in the mixture.
7. Place the baking pan in the fryer basket and cook for 25-30 minutes. To check if the cake is done: poke the center of the cake with a toothpick or metal skewer. If it comes out wet, cook it a little more.
8. Remove the baking pan from the air fryer basket and allow to cool for 10 minutes before removing from the pan.

Nutrition: Calories: 491; Fat: 25 g; Protein: 8 g; Carbs: 60 g; Fibre: 5 g; Sugar: 28 g

Chocolate and Chilli Brownies in the Airfryer

Prep Time: 15 min
Cooking Time: 15-20 min
Servings: 10

Directions
1. Preheat the air fryer to 180°C
2. Mix the butter, sugar and crushed dried chillies.
3. Beat and mix in the eggs. Add the melted chocolate and vanilla essence.
4. Gradually add the flour and cocoa powder. Mix gently, do not stir too much.
5. Using a greased or baking paper lined tin/container, pour in the mixture.
6. Cook in the air fryer for 15 to 20 minutes, checking periodically to see if the upper part does not burn; If it's cooking quickly, cover it with foil or baking paper.
7. When it's done, let it cool, then cut into smaller portions to serve.

Nutrition: Calories: 300; Fat: 22 g; Protein: 5 g; Carbs: 19 g; Fibre: 5 g; Sugar: 11 g

Ingredients
- 200 g butter, melted
- 100 g cocoa powder
- 75 g dark chocolate, melted
- 2 large eggs
- 150 g caster sugar
- 1/2 tsp vanilla essence
- 150 g self-raising flour
- 1 level tbsp crushed dried chilli flakes

Chocolate Chip Cookies

Prep Time: 10 Mins
Cooking Time: 8 Mins
Servings: 12

Ingredients
- 115 g butter, melted
- 55 g brown sugar
- 50 g caster sugar
- 1 large egg
- 1 tsp. pure vanilla extract
- 185 g plain flour
- 1/2 tsp. bicarbonate of soda
- 1/2 tsp. salt
- 120 g chocolate chips
- 35 g chopped walnuts

Directions
1. In a medium bowl, combine melted butter and sugar. Add the egg and vanilla and beat until incorporated. Add the flour, baking soda, and salt and stir until combined.
2. Place a small piece of parchment in the frying basket, making sure there is room around the edges to allow air circulation. Working in batches, using a large cookie scoop (about 3 tablespoons), scoop the batter onto parchment paper, leaving 5 cm between each cookie. Press down the batter until slightly flattened.
3. Air fry for 8 minutes at 180 °C. The cookies will turn golden brown and slightly soft.
4. Let cool for 5 minutes before serving.

Nutrition: Calories: 220; Fat: 12 g; Protein: 3 g; Carbs: 24 g; Fibre: 2.5 g; Sugar: 11 g

Cinnamon Rolls

Prep Time: 5 Mins
Cooking Time: 10 Mins
Servings: 6

Directions
1. Prepare the rolls: Line the bottom of the fryer with parchment paper and brush with butter. In a medium bowl, mix together the butter, brown sugar, cinnamon, and a large pinch of salt until smooth and fluffy.
2. On a lightly floured surface, roll out the dough into one piece . Pinch the seams and fold them in half. Roll out to a 22cm x 18cm rectangle.
3. Spread the butter mixture over the dough, leaving a 1.5cm border. Roll up the dough starting on the long side, then cut crosswise into 6 pieces.
4. Place the pieces, cut-side up, evenly spaced in the air fryer basket.
5. Set the fryer to 180°C and air fry for about 10 minutes, until they are golden brown and cooked through.
6. Prepare the frosting: In a medium bowl, beat together the cream cheese, powdered sugar, and milk. If needed, add more milk using a teaspoon to thin the glaze.
7. Spread the glaze on warm cinnamon rolls and serve.

Nutrition: Calories: 251; Fat: 8 g; Protein: 3 g; Carbs: 39 g; Fibre: 0.5 g; Sugar: 22 g

Ingredients
For The Rolls
- 2 tbsp. melted butter, plus more for brushing
- 75 g packed brown sugar
- 1/2 tsp. ground cinnamon
- Salt
- Plain flour, for surface
- 225 g ready rolled pizza dough

For The Glaze
- 50 g cream cheese, softened
- 65 g icing sugar
- 1 tbsp. whole milk, plus more if needed

Prep Time: 2 Hours
Cooking Time: 10 Mins
Servings: 6

Ingredients

For The Doughnuts
- Cooking spray
- 120 ml milk
- 50 g plus 1 tsp. caster sugar
- 1 (10 g) packet or 2 1/4 tsp. active-dry yeast
- 250 g plain flour
- 1/2 tsp. salt
- 4 tbsp. melted butter
- 1 large egg
- 1 tsp. vanilla extract

For The Vanilla Glaze
- 125 g icing sugar
- 60 ml milk
- 1/2 tsp. vanilla extract

For The Chocolate Glaze
- 95 g icing sugar
- 30 g unsweetened cocoa powder
- 3 tbsp. milk

For The Cinnamon Sugar
- 100 g caster sugar
- 2 tbsp. ground cinnamon
- 2 tbsp. melted butter

Doughnuts with Toppings

Directions

Make The Doughnuts
1. Grease a large bowl with cooking spray. Pour the milk into a small microwave-safe glass bowl or measuring cup. Microwave until warm, 40 seconds. Add 1 teaspoon sugar and stir to dissolve, then sprinkle over the yeast and allow to stand until fluffy, about 8 minutes.
2. In a medium bowl, combine flour and salt.
3. In another bowl, mix the remaining sugar, butter, egg and vanilla. Pour in the yeast mixture, mix everything, then add the dry ingredients and stir with a wooden spoon until a shaggy dough forms.
4. Turn onto a lightly floured surface and knead until elastic and slightly sticky, adding more flour a teaspoon at a time if necessary, about 5 minutes. Form a ball, then place the dough in a greased bowl and cover with a clean kitchen towel.
5. Leave the dough to rise in a warm place for about 1 hour, until doubled in size.
6. Line a large baking tray with parchment paper and lightly grease with cooking spray. Knead the dough, then roll out on a lightly floured work surface and roll out into a 1.5 cm thick rectangle.
7. Using a doughnut cutter or 7.5cm and 2.5cm biscuit cutters, pierce your donuts. Knead leftovers and punch more donuts or holes.
8. Place donuts and holes on baking trays, cover with a kitchen towel and let rise for another 40 minutes to 1 hour.
9. Grease the air fryer basket with cooking spray and add 2 donuts and 2 donut holes at a time, making sure the donuts don't touch each other. Air fry at 190°C for 6 minutes until golden brown.
10. Set on a cooling rack and repeat with the remaining dough.
11. Dip donuts in frosting (see below) or follow directions for cinnamon sugar.
12. Return to cooling rack and let set for 5 minutes before serving.

Make The Vanilla Glaze:
1. In a medium bowl whisk together icing sugar, milk, and vanilla until smooth.

Make The Chocolate Glaze:
1. In a medium bowl whisk together icing sugar, cocoa powder, and milk.

Make The Cinnamon Sugar
1. In a large shallow bowl, whisk together cinnamon and sugar. Brush doughnuts with melted butter and toss in cinnamon sugar.

Nutrition: Calories: 320; Fat: 9.5 g; Protein: 6 g; Carbs: 55 g; Fibre: 4 g; Sugar: 38 g

Shortbread Chocolate Balls

Prep Time: 4 minutes
Cooking Time: 13 minutes
Servings: 9

Ingredients
- 175 g Butter
- 75 g Caster Sugar
- 250 g Plain Flour
- 1 tsp. Vanilla Essence
- 9 Chocolate chunks
- 2 tbsp. Cocoa

Directions
1. Preheat your Air Fryer to 180°C.
2. Take a bowl and mix your sugar, flour, and cocoa.
3. Rub in the butter, knead well until you see a smooth dough.
4. Now divide into balls, place a chunk of chocolate into the centre of each one, make sure none of the chocolate chunk is showing.
5. Place your chocolate shortbread balls onto a baking sheet in your Air Fryer. Cook them at 180°C for 8 minutes and then a further 5 minutes on 160°C so that you can make sure they are cooked in the middle.
6. Serve!

Nutrition: Calories: 297; Fat: 18 g; Protein: 4 g; Carbs: 31 g; Fibre: 3.5 g; Sugar: 10 g

Lemon Biscuits

Prep Time: 5 minutes
Cooking Time: 5 minutes
Servings: 9

Directions
1. Preheat the Air Fryer to 180°C.
2. Mix flour and sugar in a bowl. Add the butter and rub it in until your mix resembles breadcrumbs. Shake your bowl regularly so that the fat bits come to the top and so that you know what you have left to rub in.
3. Add the lemon rind and juice along with the egg.
4. Combine and knead until you have lovely soft dough.
5. Roll out and cut into medium sized biscuits.
6. Place the biscuits into the Air Fryer on a baking sheet and cook for five minutes at 180°C.
7. Place on a cooling tray and sprinkle with icing sugar.

Nutrition: Calories: 205; Fat: 10 g; Protein: 3.5 g; Carbs: 26 g; Fibre: 2.5 g; Sugar: 10 g

Ingredients
- 100 g Butter
- 100 g Caster Sugar
- 225 g Self Raising Flour
- 1 Small Lemon (rind and juice)
- 1 Small Egg
- 1 tsp. Vanilla Essence

Ginger Biscuits

Prep Time: 10 minutes
Cooking Time: 16 minutes
Servings: 10-12

Ingredients
- 270 g plain flour
- 2 tsp ground ginger
- 2 tsp baking soda
- 1 tbsp cinnamon
- ½ tsp salt
- 170 g butter room temperature
- 200 g white sugar
- 1 egg
- 85 g maple syrup
- 70 g sugar for coating the cookies

Directions
1. In a large bowl, mix together the flour, ginger, baking soda, cinnamon, and salt.
2. In a second bowl, beat the butter with the sugar, egg, and maple syrup until creamy.
3. Combine the dry ingredients with the wet ones. Once everything is mixed, shape into small balls using your hands.
4. Flat each ball a little (the thicker the better!)
5. Preheat your air fryer at 150°C, and then air fry the cookies for 8 minutes at the same temperature.
6. Add 4-6 biscuits simultaneously (leaving space between each one). It is not necessary to rotate them.
7. Cook until hard on the outside but soft to touch when you press the biscuit.
8. Repeat steps 6-8 for the remaining cookies.
9. Let cool before eating and enjoy!

Nutrition: Calories 300; Fat 14 g; Protein 4 g; Carbs 45 g; Fiber 3 g; Sugar 25 g

RECIPES INDEX

A
2 Ingredient Air Fryer Pizza 55
Air Fryer Boiled Eggs 17
Apple Crumble in Air Fryer 76
Apricot and Raisin Cake 77
Aubergine with Spices 70

B
Bacon Muffins 19
Beef Wellington 41
Black Pudding (Packed) 21
Broccoli in Air Fryer 65

C
Carrot Cake in Air Fryer 78
Carrots with Simple Seasoning 66
Cauliflower in Air Fryer 71
Cheese Omelette 23
Chicken Breasts with Spices 30
Chicken Drumsticks Italian Style 27
Chicken Drumsticks with Spices 32
Chicken Kiev Balls in Air Fryer 35
Chicken Parmesan in Air Fryer 34
Chicken Thighs in Air Fryer 31
Chicken Wings in Air Fryer 28
Chickpeas Simple Recipe 69

Chimichanga 57
Chocolate and Chilli Brownies in the Airfryer 79
Chocolate Chip Cookies 80
Chunky Chips in Air Fryer 62
Cinnamon Rolls 81
Coconut Prawns with Sauce 52
Cod with Butter and Lemon 50
Cottage Pie 47
Courgette with Panko 72
Crab Cakes with Tartar Sauce 51
Creamy Mashed Potatoes 73
Crispy Chicken Nuggets 33

D
Doughnuts with Toppings 83

E
Easy Meatballs in Air Fryer 40

F
Falafel in Air Fryer 58
Fish and Chips 53
French Toast Sticks 24
Fried Bacon 15
Frozen Mozzarella Sticks 68

G

Garlic and Butter Shrimps 49
Garlic Herb Turkey Breast 37
Ginger Biscuits 86

L

Lamb Steaks 43
Lemon Biscuits 85

M

Marinated Tofu 64
Mashed Potato Pancakes 74

P

Pizza Rolls Recipe 56
Prawn Skewers with Tandoori 45

R

Roast Beef in Air Fryer 44
Roast Potatoes in Air Fryer 61

S

Salmon Fillet in Air Fryer 48
Sausage Sandwiches 20
Sausages in Air Fryer 16
Scotch Eggs 18
Shortbread Chocolate Balls 84
Simple Hamburgers 42
Simple Pork Chops 38
Spicy Curried Potato Wedges 63
Steak in Air Fryer 39

T

Tandoori Chicken Tikka Kebab 26
Tuna Patties 54
Turkey Burgers Easy Way 36

V

Vegetables Breakfast Frittata 22
Vegetables Roasted in Air Fryer 67

W

Whole Roast Chicken 29

Y

Yorkshire Puddings 60

Printed in Great Britain
by Amazon